Out and About at the NEWSPAPER

by Kitty Shea
illustrated by Zachary Trover

Special thanks to our advisers for their expertise:
Ron Bernas, Copy Editor
Detroit Free Press

Susan Kesselring, M.A., Literacy Educator
Rosemount–Apple Valley–Eagan (Minnesota) School District

PICTURE WINDOW BOOKS
Minneapolis, Minnesota

The author wishes to thank Karla Wennerstrom and Mike Hanks of Sun Newspapers in Eden Prairie, Minnesota, for their focused assistance despite the day's deadlines.

Editorial Director: Carol Jones
Managing Editor: Catherine Neitge
Creative Director: Keith Griffin
Editor: Jill Kalz
Story Consultant: Terry Flaherty
Designer: Zachary Trover
Page Production: Picture Window Books
The illustrations in this book were created digitally.

Picture Window Books
5115 Excelsior Boulevard
Suite 232
Minneapolis, MN 55416
877-845-8392
www.picturewindowbooks.com

Printed in the United States of America.

Library of Congress Cataloging-in-Publication Data
Shea, Kitty.
Out and about at the newspaper / by Kitty Shea ; illustrated by Zachary Trover.
p. cm. — (Field trips)
Includes bibliographical references and index.
ISBN 1-4048-1149-4 (hardcover)
1. Newspapers—Juvenile literature. I. Trover, Zachary. II. Title. III. Field trips
(Picture Window Books)
PN4776.S54 2006
070.1'72—dc22   2005004265

We're going on a field trip to the newspaper. We can't wait!

Things to find out:

Where does the newspaper get its news?

Who writes the stories in the newspaper?

Why do people buy ads?

How do readers get the newspaper?

SHARING IS CARING

Welcome! My name is Karla. I'm the editor of the *Daily Journal*.

So, how many of you started your day with a cup of coffee and the newspaper? Just kidding. A lot of grown-ups do that. They read the newspaper to learn what's going on locally and throughout the world.

Young people need to know about current events, too. That's why I'm happy you're here today to learn about newspapers.

The newspaper is filled with new information. That's why it's called a "newspaper." Newspapers may be printed every day, a few times a week, once a week, once every two weeks, or even once a month.

5

As the editor, I decide what goes into the *Daily Journal*. Sometimes, people call or write to tell me what's new. Other times, they call the reporters. I pick stories that I think our readers will find important or interesting.

There are two kinds of stories in newspapers: news stories and feature stories. News stories are about real people, places, and happenings. People read them to learn about the world. Feature stories can be about anything. People read them for entertainment and enjoyment.

Reporters write the stories that go in the newspaper. I assign stories to them like your teacher assigns homework to you. I correct their stories, too!

EDITORIAL

Reporters interview their sources to find out the facts. Then, they write their stories on computers here in the newsroom.

Reporters are very curious. They ask a lot of questions and listen carefully to the answers. Reporters may go to the library or use the Internet to learn more facts.

9

Mike is one of our reporters. He's on deadline, which means he must finish his story by a certain time. Mike is writing about the Penny Project. The Penny Project was started by kids from Shorewood Elementary. They heard that the fire department needed new portable radios. They raised money, penny by penny, to help the fire department buy them.

All reporters use the five Ws to gather information about a story: who, what, where, when, and why.

WHO
Students at Shorewood Elementary School

WHAT
Donated money raised through Penny Project

WHERE
Station 74

WHEN
Last Thursday

WHY
Buy new portable radios

Readers expect to learn basic information from any story in the newspaper. They want to know the "who, what, where, when, and why." Reporters put this information in the lead, or the beginning, of the story.

We have show-and-tell here, just like you have in school. Newspapers show pictures and tell stories. Rick is our photographer. He takes pictures of local people and events.

He took a picture of the Penny Project kids giving the fire chief the money they raised. The photo will be in tomorrow's newspaper next to Mike's story.

Photographers use a lot of equipment. After taking a picture, they can make it lighter or darker on the computer. They can also cut off the edges of a picture. This is called cropping. It helps readers focus on what's important.

It costs money to publish a newspaper. We make money by selling advertising, or space, in the newspaper. Businesses fill the space with ads. Big ads cost more than small ads. Businesses use ads to sell their products or services.

You or I can buy an ad, too. For example, if you've outgrown your bike, you might buy an ad that reads "Bike for sale!"

The stories are written. The pictures are taken. The ads are sold. Now our design editor must fit all of the pieces onto the page. It's a little like putting together a puzzle. When everything is in the right place, the newspaper should look nice and be easy to read.

Masthead

Headline

Byline

Body Copy

Photo

Daily Journal

Volume 23, Issue 16, 75¢

Penny Project Helps Fire Department

By Mike Hanks, Staff Reporter

Children from Shorewood Elementary School present the $1,107.89 they collected during the Penny Project to Dick Sutton, Fire Chief of Station 74.

Caption

Newspapers group stories into sections so people can find them easily. Sections may include local news, world news, sports, and entertainment. Most newspapers also have comics, TV listings, and letters from readers.

Because we are a big newspaper, we have our own printing presses.

Can you hear me okay? It gets very loud in here when the presses are running.

The presses put the ink on the paper. The blank paper goes in one end, and the printed newspaper comes out the other end.

When people buy a subscription, they pay for a certain number of issues of the newspaper. The newspaper is then delivered to their homes or workplaces. Some people buy the newspaper at stores or newsstands, or read it at the public library.

Here's a copy of the *Daily Journal* for you to take home. Practice your reading skills by reading the newspaper. Maybe one day we'll see a story in here about you!

PUBLISHING YOUR OWN NEWSPAPER

What kinds of things are you and your class doing? Share the news with others in school by making your own monthly class newspaper!

What you need:

a variety of newspapers	a computer with word processing software (optional)
pencils or pens	a computer printer (optional)
notebooks	two sheets of 11- x17-inch (28- x 43-centimeter) paper
white paper	glue
at least one camera	a copy machine

What you do:

1. Name the newspaper.

2. Look at sample newspapers to get ideas for different sections. Your class newspaper, for example, could include a main news story, a feature story, the school lunch menu, and pictures of classmates doing things in school.

3. Decide what to write about for the main news and feature stories. Who will be the sources? What facts need to be gathered? Write down the questions you need to ask the sources.

4. Interview the sources. Listen carefully and take notes as they answer your questions.

5. Write the stories. Remember to include the "who, what, where, when, and why" in the lead sentence or paragraph. Your teacher (the editor) should read the stories to make sure they have all the facts and tell the whole story.

6. Recopy the corrected stories in columns by hand or use a computer. Use a real newspaper as a guide.

7. Take pictures that show what the stories are about. Print the best pictures out on the printer or take the film to a photo shop for developing.

8. Make a masthead on a piece of white paper. The masthead includes your paper's name and should fill the top part of one of the big sheets of paper.

9. Place all the stories and pictures on the big sheets of paper. Leave room for headlines above stories and captions below pictures. Write headlines and captions on white paper, either by hand or on the computer. When everything is in place, glue the pieces down.

10. Ask your teacher to help you photocopy the correct number of sheets. Put the newspapers together and deliver them to other classrooms.

FUN FACTS

- Newspapers can publish whatever they want, as long as it's the truth. This is called "freedom of the press." It's part of the First Amendment to the United States Constitution.

- More than half of all adults in the United States read a newspaper every day. Most people read the news about world and national events first, then the local news, entertainment stories, sports scores, and comics.

- Newsboys in the early 20th century stood on city street corners and yelled "Extra! Extra! Read all about it!" They did this to try to sell newspapers to people passing by. The word "extra" meant that the newspaper had just come off the printing press and contained the most up-to-date news.

- More than nine million tons (8 million metric tons) of old newspapers are recycled each year. Most of them are turned back into newspapers. The rest of them become cereal boxes, egg cartons, grocery bags, tissue paper, and even bedding for farm animals.

GLOSSARY

advertising—space in the newspaper that businesses buy to tell readers about their products or services

byline—the name of the reporter who wrote the story; the byline appears under the headline

caption—the information that appears beneath a photo and tells what is happening in the photo; a caption is also called a cutline

deadline—the time by which stories, photos, and ads need to be completed and turned in

facts—things that have actually happened, or information that is truthful and correct

interview—to ask questions of a source either in person or on the telephone or computer

lead—the first sentence or paragraph of a story; the lead (LEED) has the basic facts about the story

publish—to create a newspaper or other printed form of communication and make it available to the public

sources—people from whom a reporter learns the facts about a story

TO LEARN MORE

At the Library

Anderson, Catherine. *Newspaper*. Chicago: Heinemann Library, 2005.

Christian, Sandra J. *Newspaper Carriers*. Mankato, Minn.: Bridgestone Books, 2002.

Englart, Mindi Rose. *Newspapers from Start to Finish*. San Diego: Blackbirch Press, 2001.

Gish, Melissa. *A Newspaper*. North Mankato, Minn.: Smart Apple Media, 2003.

On the Web

FactHound offers a safe, fun way to find Web sites related to this book. All of the sites on FactHound have been researched by our staff. *www.facthound.com*

1. Visit the FactHound home page.
2. Enter a search word related to this book, or type in this special code: 1404811494.
3. Click on the FETCH IT button.

Your trusty FactHound will fetch the best sites for you!

INDEX

Look for all the books in the Field Trips series:

Out and About at ...